# Toronto Adventures
## with the Cousins!

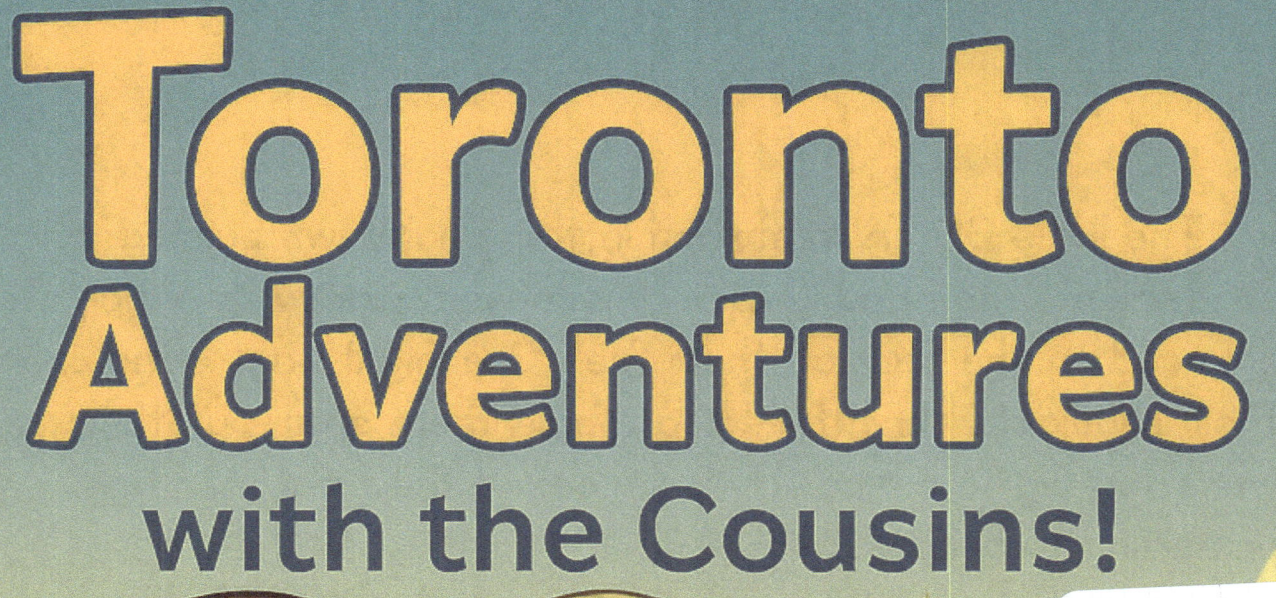

By Christine Leger

The little GO Train station in the small town buzzed with excitement! Toby and Charlie, their eyes wide with anticipation, bounced on the balls of their feet. Overnight bags slung over their shoulders threatened to topple them over, but their grins were too big to notice. They squeezed their parents tight, promising to behave.

"Have fun, and take lots of pictures!" said Uncle Mark, ruffling Toby's already messy hair.

"And don't forget your toothbrushes!" added Ma Tante Sophie with a playful wink.

Then, with a whoosh and a soft roar, the train pulled into the station, its doors hissing a welcome. Standing in the open doorway, waving frantically, were Olivia and Edmund!

"Toronto, here we come!" Edmund grinned, his eyes sparkling.

Behind them stood Mom, Memere, and Pepere, a symphony of rolling suitcases and even wider smiles. The Toronto adventure was about to begin!

The GO Train was a magical zooming machine! It whisked them past endless green fields dotted with cows, sleepy little towns, and busy highways crowded with cars. Inside, the cousins were a whirlwind of activity.

They munched on snacks (mostly cookies, thanks to Memere), played a noisy game of cards (Olivia was a surprisingly good cheat!), and pointed out Lake Ontario as the majestic skyline of Toronto began to peek over the horizon. Excitement crackled in the air like static electricity, making them all giggle uncontrollably.

Their first adventure? Ripley's Aquarium! Stepping into the underwater tunnel was like entering a different world. Sharks glided silently overhead, their shadows menacing. Jellyfish pulsed with ethereal light, their tentacles dancing in a hypnotic rhythm.

Toby squealed with delight, pointing at a tiny clownfish hiding in a coral reef. Pepere, however, was completely captivated by the graceful stingrays, their bodies rippling as they swam by, almost seeming to smile. They spent hours exploring the depths, mesmerized by the incredible creatures of the sea.

Next, it was time to conquer the CN Tower! The elevator zipped upwards so fast that Olivia felt her stomach tickle. At the top, the view was breathtaking! The city stretched out below them like a giant toy set.

Olivia, ever the daredevil, pressed her face right against the glass floor, giggling as she looked down at the dizzying drop. Charlie, on the other hand, scooted as far away from the edge as possible, his eyes wide with a mixture of fear and wonder.

"It's like flying!" exclaimed Edmund, spreading his arms like wings. Memere, always prepared with her camera, snapped a group photo with the magnificent skyline as their backdrop.

A short ferry ride transported them to the peaceful oasis of Toronto Island. Leaving the city noise behind, they found themselves surrounded by lush green parks, sandy beaches, and the gentle lapping of the waves.

Toby and Edmund, always competitive, embarked on a stone-skipping competition, their arms windmilling as they tried to beat each other's record. Olivia and Charlie, more interested in nature, sat by the shore weaving daisy chains, their fingers nimble as they created colorful crowns.

Before heading back to the city, they shared sticky, dripping popsicles, their faces stained with sugary sweetness.

As evening approached, a very special dinner awaited them: Medieval Times! The arena was a riot of colour and sound, filled with knights on horseback, waving flags, and the roar of cheering crowds. They were seated in their assigned section, eagerly awaiting the show.

The knights jousted and fought with swords, showcasing their impressive skills. And the best part? They ate their dinner with their hands – no forks allowed! "This is the loudest dinner ever," laughed Mom, wiping some stray gravy from her cheek. It was a truly unforgettable experience.

The next morning began with a trip to Casa Loma, a magnificent castle that seemed straight out of a fairytale. The cousins transformed into royal adventurers, racing through secret tunnels, exploring hidden passageways, and discovering grand ballrooms.

Charlie, declaring himself the lord of the castle, claimed a turret as his "dragon tower," imagining himself battling imaginary foes. They spent hours lost in the magic of the castle, their imaginations running wild.

The Royal Ontario Museum – or ROM – was their next stop. Dinosaur bones towered above them, casting long shadows. "I'm glad these ones aren't alive," whispered Toby, clutching Edmund's arm. They wandered through halls filled with ancient artifacts from around the world, marveling at the history contained within the museum walls.

The best part was the hands-on exhibits, where they could touch and interact with replicas of ancient tools and objects. They learned so much, and had fun doing it!

Then, a visit to Little Canada, a miniature world that sparkled with lights and tiny trains. The detail was incredible! Replicas of famous Canadian landmarks were meticulously crafted, complete with miniature people and moving vehicles. "Look! It's Ottawa – but mini!" shouted Olivia, pointing excitedly at a tiny replica of Parliament Hill.

They spent ages exploring the miniature cities, spotting familiar landmarks and marvelling at the craftsmanship.

The day concluded with an exciting trip to the Rogers Centre to cheer on Memere's favourite team: the Toronto Blue Jays! The stadium was a sea of blue, filled with roaring fans and the smell of hot dogs. The cousins, armed with giant foam fingers and wearing Blue Jays hats, joined in the cheering, their voices hoarse by the end of the game.

Memere wore her lucky cap, convinced that it would bring the team good luck. "We might be their good luck charm!" said Edmund, his eyes sparkling with excitement.

Tired but smiling, they boarded the GO Train for the journey back to their cousins' small town. The day had been packed with adventure, and they were all exhausted. "That was the BEST two days ever," said Charlie, already starting to doze off against Olivia's shoulder.

"We saw so much," agreed Olivia, her voice soft with contentment. The memories of their Toronto adventures danced in their heads as the train rumbled through the night.

But the fun wasn't quite over yet! On the drive back to Ottawa, Mom surprised Edmund and Olivia with a detour to the Toronto Zoo. Their faces lit up with excitement! "We'll say hi to every animal!" Olivia insisted, grabbing her brother's hand and dragging him towards the entrance.

From playful pandas to majestic lions, the zoo was a wonderland of creatures, waiting to be discovered.

As the car rolled back into Ottawa, Olivia sighed contentedly. "We have to go back," she said, her voice full of longing. "For what?" Edmund asked, stifling a yawn. "The Santa Claus Parade! And the Christmas Market in the Distillery District!" she beamed, her eyes sparkling with anticipation.

"Next time," Mom smiled in the rearview mirror, her voice warm with promise. The Toronto adventures had only just begun!

Thanks for exploring
Toronto with us!
Until next time -O&E